This copy of

The Warty Witches'
Joke Book

belongs to

Wi

Also available in Beaver by John Hegarty

Clever Dick
A Jumble of Jungly Jokes
Not the Elephant Joke Book
A Very Mice Joke Book

The Warty Witches' Joke Book

John Hegarty

Illustrated by Jean Baylis

BEAVER BOOKS

A Beaver Book
Published by Arrow Books Limited
62–5 Chandos Place, London WC2N 4NW

An imprint of Century Hutchinson Ltd

London Melbourne Sydney Auckland
Johannesburg and agencies throughout the world

First published in 1989

Set in Century Schoolbook
by JH Graphics Ltd, Reading

Made and printed in Great Britain
by Courier International
Tiptree, Essex

ISBN 0 09 962140 1

Warty Witches and Co.

What is a warty witch's favourite magazine?
The Witch Report!

What is a young warty witch's favourite TV programme?
Strange Hill.

How can you tell if a warty witch has a glass eye?
When it comes out in conversation.

What goes cackle, cackle, bonk?
A warty witch laughing her head off.

The warty witches' motto: *We came, We saw, We conjured.*

How can you make a witch itch?
Take away her W.

What did the doctor say to the warty witch?
Tomorrow you'll be able to get out of bed for a spell.

Why did the young warty witch have such difficulty writing letters?
She'd never learnt to spell properly.

What do you call a warty wizard from outer space?
A flying sorcerer.

What do you call a motorbike belonging to a warty witch?
A baaarrooooom stick!

What do you get if you cross a warty witch with a werewolf?
A mad dog that chases aeroplanes.

What do you get if you cross a sorceress with a millionaire?
A vewy witch person.

What kind of tests do they give in warty witch school?
Hex-aminations.

How do warty witches on broomsticks drink their tea?
Out of flying saucers.

Where does a warty witch keep her purse?
In her hag bag.

What do warty witches ring for in a hotel?
B-room service.

What kind of jewellery do warty witches wear on their wrists?
Charm bracelets.

Why did the warty witch give up her job as a fortune-teller?
She couldn't see much future in it.

What do warty witches say when they overtake each other?
'Broom broom broom!'

What's the difference between a deer running away and a small warty witch?
One's a hunted stag and the other's a stunted hag.

What happened when the old warty witch went to see a funny film?
The manager told her to cut the cackle.

What do you call a hag that stops cars with her thumb?
A witch hiker.

What happens to a warty witch when she loses her temper riding her broomstick?
She flies off the handle.

What are baby warty witches called?
Halloweenies.

Why do warty witches get good bargains?
Because they like to haggle.

What happens if you are confronted with two identical hags?
You can't tell witch is witch.

Why do warty wizards drink tea?
Because sorcerers need cuppas.

Why didn't the warty witch sing at the concert?
Because she had a frog in her throat.

What do you call a warty witch who drives really badly?
A road hag.

1ST WARTY WITCH: I'm going to cast a spell and make myself beautiful. I'll have hundreds of men at my feet.
2ND WARTY WITCH: *Yes, chiropodists.*

What happens to warty witches when it rains?
They get wet.

WARTY WITCH TO SHOPKEEPER: How much are
   your black candles?
SHOPKEEPER: *A pound each.*
WARTY WITCH: That's candleous!

What is black and ugly and has eight wheels?
A warty witch on roller skates.

Why won't a warty witch wear a flat hat?
Because there's no point in it.

What do you call a warty witch that stays out all night?
A fresh air freak.

What do you get if you cross a warty witch with an iceberg?
A cold spell.

Why is the air so clean and healthy on Halloween?
Because so many warty witches are sweeping the sky.

What's the favourite subject of young warty witch school kids?
Spelling, of course!

Why did the warty witch consult an astrologer?
She wanted to know her horror-scope.

What's the difference between a warty witch and the letters M, A, K, E, S?
One makes spells and the other spells makes.

What do warty children do after school?
Their gnomework.

Why do warty witches ride on broomsticks?
It beats walking.

What is the warty witches' favourite musical?
My Fear Lady.

What happened when the boy warty wizard met the girl warty witch?
It was love at first fright.

What's the best thing to do if you find a warty witch in your bed?
Run!

What happened to the naughty witch schoolgirl?
She was ex-spelled.

What does a warty witch chef enjoy cooking most?
Gnomelettes!

How do baby warty witches cry?
Brew-hoo! Brew-hoo!

Why should men be careful of beautiful warty witches?
They'll sweep them off their feet.

Is it true that a warty witch won't hurt you if you run away from her?
It all depends on how fast you run!

What do you call a warty witch who kills her mother and father?
An orphan.

What's yellow and highly dangerous?
Witch-infested custard!

Who won the warty witches' beauty contest?
No one!

How can you tell when warty witches are carrying a time bomb?
You can hear their brooms tick!

How do warty witches keep their hair out of place?
With scare spray.

Did you hear about the warty wizard who can sculpt all kinds of things from old skull-bones?
He is said to have a high degree of witchcraftsmanship

How is an evil warty witch like a candle?
They are both wick-ed.

WARTY WITCH: What would you like for your birthday, darling?
WIZARD: *Something to match the colour of my eyes.*
WARTY WITCH: But where can I find a bloodshot tie?

What is the warty witches' favourite slogan?
Please Give Blood Generously.

Why did the warty witch tiptoe past the medicine cabinet?
She didn't want to wake the sleeping pills.

Did you hear about the warty wizard who fell into a barrel of beer?
He came to a bitter end.

What do you call a nervous sorceress?
A twitch.

What's the difference between a musician and a dead witch?
One composes and the other decomposes.

What do you call a warty witch with one leg?
Eileen.

What do you get if you cross an owl with a warty witch?
A bird that's ugly but doesn't give a hoot.

Why did the warty witch go to the psychiatrist?
Because she thought everybody loved her.

Which of the warty witches' friends eats the fastest?
The goblin.

Warty witch graffiti:

SAY IT WITH FLOWERS – GIVE HER A TRIFFID

'Doctor, doctor, you must help me!'
'What's the problem?'
'Every night, I dream there are thousands of warty witches under my bed. What on earth can I do?'
'Saw the legs off your bed.'

When the picture of the warty witch's grandfather crashed to the floor in the middle of the night, what did it mean?
That the nail had come out of the wall.

What is the most comfortable way to see a warty witch?
On television.

A warty witch was so lonely that she wrote off to a Lonely Hearts Club to find herself a man friend. Soon she got a letter back, and she started quite a friendship with the man by post. Eventually they decided to meet. 'I haven't mentioned this before,' the witch wrote, 'but I'm very old and ugly and love pets that are covered in slime and thick hair. I smell very bad from standing over my cauldron of witch's brew all day, and I do tend to cackle a lot. If this doesn't put you off too much, let's meet under the clock at Waterloo Station next Sunday, at 2 o'clock.'

'My dear lady,' her friend wrote back, 'I couldn't care less about your looks. Your personality and our friendship are much more important to me. In fact I really look forward to seeing you — but will you please wear a red carnation and carry a copy of the *Financial Times*, to help me recognize you?'

What did the warty wizard write on his Christmas cards?
Best vicious of the season.

If a warty wizard was knocked out by Dracula, what would he be?
Out for the Count.

'I bet I can get you to forget about the warty witch?'
'What warty witch?'
'See — you've forgotten already.'

Could you kill a warty witch just by throwing eggs at her?
Of course, she'd be eggs-terminated.

What does a warty witch do if her broom is stolen?
Call the Flying Squad.

What's old and ugly and goes beep beep?
A warty witch in a traffic jam.

What do you get if you cross King Kong with a warty witch's toad?
A monster that climbs up the Empire State Building and catches aeroplanes with its tongue.

WARTY WITCH: Doctor, doctor, you've got to help me – I keep dreaming of bats, creepy-crawlies, demons, ghosts, monsters, vampires, werewolves and yetis . . .
DOCTOR: *How very interesting! Do you always dream in alphabetical order?*

WARTY WITCH: Will you love me when I'm old and ugly?
WARTY WIZARD: *Darling, of course I do.*

1ST WARTY WITCH: Why do you keep throwing bunches of garlic out of the window?

2ND WARTY WITCH: *To keep the vampires away.*

1ST WARTY WITCH: But there are no vampires around here.

2ND WARTY WITCH: *Jolly effective, isn't it?*

What is old and ugly and hangs on the line?
A drip-dry warty witch.

A man went into a pub with a big, vicious looking Rottweiler on a lead. 'Sorry, sir,' said the barman, 'but that creature looks dangerous. You'll have to tie him up outside.' So the man took the Rottweiler outside, and came back and ordered a drink. He was just finishing it when a warty witch came into the bar and said, 'Whose Rottweiler is that outside?' 'Mine,' said the man, beaming with pride. 'Well, I'm sorry,' the warty witch said, 'but my little pet's just killed him.' ' "Killed him"? What kind of little pet do you have?' 'A cat,' said the warty witch. 'But how could a cat kill my great big Rottweiler?' 'She got stuck in his throat and choked him.'

How do you know when you're in bed with a warty witch?
Because she's got a big 'WW' on her pyjamas.

When should you feed witch's milk to a baby?
When it's a baby witch.

What is a warty witch after she is one year old?
A two-year-old warty witch.

A very posh lady was walking around an art
gallery, when she stopped by one particular
exhibit. 'I suppose this picture of a hideous warty
witch is what you call modern art,' she said very
pompously.

'No, madam,' replied the assistant, 'that's what
we call a mirror.'

Did you hear about the very well-behaved little
warty wizard? When he was good his father would
give him a penny and a pat on the head. By the
time he was sixteen he had £25 in the bank and
his head was totally flat!

A gang of warty witches broke into a blood bank
last night and stole a thousand pints of blood.
Police are still hunting for the clots.

The warty witch mother had such an ugly baby she didn't push the pram – she pulled it.

What do you call a warty witch who climbs up walls?
Ivy.

Where do the cleanest warty witches live?
Bath.

Did you hear about the warty witch who went on a crash diet?
She wrecked three cars and a motorbike.

What do you call a warty wizard who lies on the floor all the time?
Matt.

At a party an old warty witch was complaining about the appearance and behaviour of modern warty witches.

'Look at that girl over there,' she said. 'She's wearing a boy's shirt, a boy's jeans, and she's got a boy's haircut instead of long straggly rats' tails – it's hard to tell she's a girl at all.'

'As it happens,' came the reply, 'that *is* a girl, and I should know, because she's my daughter.'

'I'm so sorry,' said the old warty witch. 'I just didn't realize you were her father.'

'I'm not. I'm her mother.'

What do you call a warty wizard who's black and blue all over?
Bruce.

TEACHER: In the warty witch's coven, there was the mother, the father, the grandmother and the little baby. How many does that make?
WARTY WITCH PUPIL: *Three — and one to carry.*

How do you keep an ugly warty witch in suspense?
I'll tell you tomorrow . . .

Why does a warty wizard clean his teeth three times a day?
To prevent bat breath.

What happened to the warty witch who ran away with the circus?
The police made her bring it back.

What do you call a warty wizard who has fallen into the sea in a barrel?
Bob.

What do you call a warty wizard who's been dead and buried for a million years?
Pete.

How does a warty witch make scrambled eggs?
She holds the pan and gets two friends to make the stove shake with fright.

Where is the warty witch's temple?
On the side of her head.

What do you call a warty wizard lying in the gutter?
Dwayne.

What do you call a warty wizard who sits on a bonfire?
Guy.

Where do warty witches go for their holidays?
Bat-lins.

Who did the warty wizard marry?
His ghoul-friend.

Why do some warty witches eat raw meat?
Because they don't know how to cook.

How do you make a warty witch float?
Take two scoops of ice cream, a glass of Coke and add one warty witch.

From the Warty Witches' Library:

Never Make a Warty Witch Angry by Sheila Tack
The Vampire's Victim by E. Drew Blood
Chased by a Werewolf by Claude Bottom
The Omen by B. Warned
Foaming at the Mouth by Dee Monic
Wizard from Another Planet by A. Lee-En
I saw a Warty Witch by Denise R. Knockin
In the Warty Witch's Cauldron by Mandy Ceased
Boo! by Terry Fie
The Warty Witch meets Dracula by Pearce Nex
The Ghost of the Warty Witch by Eve L. Spirit
Black Magic by Sue Pernatural
Witch's Coven by De Ville Worshipper
Terrible Spells by B. Witcher.

What do you get if you cross a warty witch's cat
with Father Christmas?
Santa Claws.

What's the name of the warty wizard's cook?
Fangy Craddock.

How do warty witches know that S is a scary letter?
Because it makes cream scream.

WARTY WIZARD BOY: What would I have to give you to get a little kiss?
WARTY WITCH GIRL: *Chloroform.*

What sort of soup do warty wizards like?
One with plenty of body in it.

Did you hear about the stupid warty wizard?
He thought 'the great smell of Brut' was the Incredible Hulk's BO!

Did you hear about the warty witch that has pedestrian eyes?
They look both ways before they cross.

1ST WARTY WIZARD: I don't think much of your pet toad.

2ND WARTY WIZARD: *Never mind — eat the vegetables instead.*

What do you get if you cross a warty witch with a flea?
Lots of very worried dogs.

What is old and ugly and very blue?
A warty witch holding her breath.

If you saw nine warty witches outside Woolworth's
in black capes and one warty witch outside Boots
in a blood red cape, what would that prove?
That nine out of ten warty witches wear black capes.

WITCH IN SHOP: I'm looking for something to make
my rock cakes light.
SHOP ASSISTANT: *I'm afraid we don't sell petrol,
madam.*

1ST WARTY WITCH: Your little daughter's grown!
2ND WARTY WITCH: *Oh yes, she's certainly
gruesome.*

WARTY WITCH: You should keep control of your little boy. He just bit me on the ankle.

VILE VAMPIRE: *That's only because he couldn't reach your neck.*

1ST WARTY WITCH: Have you tried one of those paper cauldrons?

2ND WARTY WITCH: *Yes.*

1ST WARTY WITCH: Did it work?

2ND WARTY WITCH: *No, it was tearable.*

1ST WARTY WITCH: Shall I buy black or white candles?

2ND WARTY WITCH: *Which burn longer?*

1ST WARTY WITCH: Neither, they both burn shorter.

What should you expect if you call unexpectedly on a warty witch at lunchtime?
Pot luck.

WARTY WITCH: I'm never coming to this restaurant again — my friend here has just swallowed a live frog!
WAITER: *Does she feel ill?*
WARTY WITCH: Ill? She'll croak at any minute!

What do warty witches like to eat for breakfast?
Rice Krispies, because they go snap, cackle and pop!

What do warty witches like best for lunch?
Real toad in the hole.

1ST WARTY WITCH: I'm going to France tomorrow.
2ND WARTY WITCH: *Are you going by broom?*
1ST WARTY WITCH: No, by Hoovercraft.

What is the best way of stopping infection from warty witch bites?
Don't bite any warty witches.

WARTY WITCH IN PET SHOP: I've got a complaint. This toad you sold me keeps bumping into things.

PET SHOP ASSISTANT: *I expect he needs glasses.*

WARTY WITCH: But I can't afford to send him to the hoptician!

WARTY WITCH: I'd like some new tiles for my bathroom.

ASSISTANT: *But madam, this is a pet shop.*

WARTY WITCH: That's all right — I want reptiles.

Did you hear about the warty witch's stupid pet werewolf?
It lay down to chew a bone, and when it got up it had only three legs.

What kind of music do warty witches play on the piano?
Hag-time

What's old, ugly and can see just as well from both ends?
A warty witch wearing a blindfold.

Did you hear about the warty witch who wasn't pretty and wasn't ugly?
She was pretty ugly.

Why do warty witches ride on broomsticks?
Because vacuum cleaners are too heavy.

What do you call a wicked old woman who lives by the sea?
A sand-witch.

How do witches drink tea?
With cups and sorcerers.

Why do little warty witches always get As at school?
Because they're so good at spelling.

What is a warty witch's favourite TV programme?
Horror-nation Street.

How do you stop a warty witch's pet werewolf from attacking you?
Throw a stick and shout, 'Fetch, boy!'

What do you call a friendly and handsome warty witch?
A failure.

What is the best thing to do if a warty witch comes in through your front door?
Run out of the back door.

What kinds of warty witches have their eyes closest together?
The smallest ones, of course!

What must a warty witch be to receive a state funeral?
Dead.

What kinds of warty witches can jump higher than a house?
All kinds — houses can't jump.

Why are warty witches' finger nails never more than eleven inches long?
Because if they were twelve inches they'd be a foot.

What do you call a warty witch who rides first class in a jumbo-jet?
A passenger.

What do you call a warty witch who has written a book?
An author.

'What is evil and ugly, puts spells on people, and is made of cement?'
'What?'
'A warty witch.'
'But what about the cement?'
'I just threw that in to make it hard!'

What do you do with a blue warty witch?
Try to cheer her up.

What does a warty witch turn into when the lights go out?
The dark.

TEACHER: If you saw me standing by a warty witch, what fruit would it remind you of?

PUPIL: *A pear.*

Why do warty witches go to Earl's Court?
To visit the Bat Show, of course!

1ST WARTY WITCH: What is that son of yours doing these days?

2ND WARTY WITCH: *He's at medical school.*

1ST WARTY WITCH: Oh. What's he studying?

2ND WARTY WITCH: *Nothing. They're studying him.*

1ST WARTY WITCH: I took my husband to the zoo yesterday.
2ND WARTY WITCH: *Did they accept him?*

1ST WARTY WIZARD: I took my wife to the beauty parlour yesterday. I was waiting for three hours while they attended to her.
2ND WARTY WIZARD: *Did she look any better afterwards?*
1ST WARTY WIZARD: Oh, she didn't have anything done. She only went for an estimate.

What makes more noise than an angry warty witch?
Two angry warty witches.

Little Nigel was on a train with his mother when suddenly he started to whisper in her ear.

'Nigel,' said his mother crossly, 'how many times have I told you it's rude to whisper. If you've got something to say, say it out loud.'

'All right,' said Nigel, 'why has that woman got a face like a ten ton warty witch?

1ST WARTY WIZARD: My mother-in-law is so ugly, that when a tear rolls down her cheek it takes one look at her face and rolls straight back up again.

2ND WARTY WIZARD: Count yourself lucky. My mother-in-law is so ugly, she can make her own yoghurt just by staring at a bottle of milk for a couple of minutes.

Did you hear about the man who took up witch-hunting for a living?
He used to be a teacher, but he lost his nerve.

A warty witch walked into a beauty salon and asked the beautician: 'How can I be made to look like a film star?'

The beautician looked at the witch and said, 'May I suggest that you either visit the plastic surgeon next door, or that you stay as you are.'

'How can I stay as I am and still look like a film star?' asked the warty witch.

'Didn't you ever see *The Creature from the Black Lagoon?*'

DOCTOR: Did the mudpack help your appearance?
WARTY WITCH PATIENT: *It did, but it fell off after a few days.*

BOY WARTY WIZARD: Dad, the boy next door said I look just like you.
DAD WARTY WIZARD: *What did you say?*
BOY WARTY WIZARD: Nothing. He's bigger than me.

DOCTOR: What's the trouble?
WARTY WITCH PATIENT: *I can't stop pulling ugly faces.*
DOCTOR: That's nothing to worry about.
WARTY WITCH PATIENT: *But people with ugly faces don't like them being pulled.*

Did you hear about the baby warty witch?
It was so ugly, its parents ran away from home.

HUMAN PATIENT (*on the telephone*): Doctor, there's something terribly wrong with me. My head feels squashed, my voice sounds strange, I keep smelling something really awful, and one of my feet is cold. Have I turned into a warty witch?

DOCTOR: *Don't worry. You're probably wearing one of your socks on your head.*

WARTY WIZARD BROTHER: You've got a Roman nose.

WARTY WITCH SISTER: *Like Julius Caesar, you mean?*

WARTY WITCH BROTHER: No, it's roamin' all over your face.

TV PRODUCER: Is the warty witch actress good looking?

TV DIRECTOR: *Well let's put it this way: she's got a perfect face for radio.*

JOHNNY: Are you having a party for your birthday?

JIMMY: *No, I'm having a warty witch do!*

JOHNNY: What's a warty witch do?

JIMMY: *It goes around being mean and ugly and putting spells on people!*

WARTY WITCH MOTHER TO WARTY WIZARD SON: When your grandfather was born they passed out cigars. When your father was born they passed out cigarettes. When you were born — they just passed out.

POLICEMAN (*studying photograph*): Is this a true likeness of your missing husband?

WARTY WITCH: *Yes it is.*

POLICEMAN: In that case, we'll start by searching the zoo.

1ST WARTY WITCH GIRL: I spend ages in front of the mirror admiring my beauty. Do you think it's vanity?

2ND WARTY WITCH GIRL: *No. Imagination.*

WARTY WITCH: I have the face of a sixteen year old girl.

WARTY WIZARD BOY: *Well you'd better give it back then. You're getting it all wrinkled.*

1ST WARTY WITCH: What's your new boyfriend like?

2ND WARTY WITCH: *He is mean, nasty, ugly, smelly, and totally evil — but he has some bad points, too.*

TEACHER: What would you do if you saw a big warty witch?

PUPIL: *Hope she didn't see me!*

BOY WARTY WIZARD: I'm so glad you named me Gunge-zilla.

MOTHER WARTY WITCH: *Why?*

BOY WARTY WIZARD: Because that's what all the kids at school call me.

WARTY WITCH: Did you ever see anyone like me before?

HUMAN GIRL: *Yes, once. But I had to pay admission.*

What do warty witches sing at Christmas?
'Deck the halls with poison ivy . . .'

A sea-witch heard the sound of moaning and groaning on the sea-bed, and discovered a squid with stomach ache. 'Ooooh,' sighed the squid, 'I've been vomiting all night.'

'Have you seen a doctor?' asked the sea-witch. 'No,' said the squid.

'Well come with me,' said the witch, 'I have a friend who can help you.' So the witch took one of the squid's tentacles and led him gently to the surface, where a large whale was quietly resting and blowing water through his spout. The witch guided the squid over to the whale, and said, 'Here you go, Fred — here's that sick squid I owe you.'

Did you hear about the warty witch with the upside down nose?
Every time she sneezed, her hat blew off.

1ST WARTY WIZARD: My wife's beauty is timeless.
2ND WARTY WIZARD: *Oh, you mean her face could stop a clock?*

Why did the warty witch jump from the top of the Empire State Building?
Because she wanted to make a hit on Broadway.

What do you do if a warty witch in a pointed hat sits in front of you at the cinema?
Miss most of the film!

WARTY WIZARD: My wife's got a face like a million dollars – all green and wrinkled!

Why did the warty witch buy two tickets to the zoo?
One to get in, and one to get out.

How do you make a witch stew?
Keep her waiting for a few hours.

What do little warty witches play with?
Deady bears.

What did the warty wizard say to the warty witch?
'Hi, gore-juice!'

1ST HUMAN BOY: My dad saw a horrible warty witch and didn't turn a hair.
2ND HUMAN BOY: *I'm not surprised – your dad's bald!*

Why did the warty wizard wear red, white and blue braces?
To keep his trousers up.

If a warty witch keeps watching Mickey Mouse films, what's up with her?
She's having Disney spells.

Why do some warty witches have Big Ears?
Because Noddy won't pay the ransom.

Why did the warty witch wear yellow stockings?
Because her grey ones were at the laundry.

What goes cackle, cackle, squelch, squelch?
A warty witch in soggy plimsolls.

What usually runs in the warty witch family?
Noses.

What goes cackle, cackle, bang?
A warty witch in a minefield.

Why does a warty witch wear open-toed sandals?
To go to the beach.

A workman had just finished laying a huge wall-to-wall carpet in the warty witch's cave when he noticed a small lump in the centre. 'So that's where I left my cigarettes,' he said. 'I was wondering where they had got to.' Rather than take up the whole carpet and have to lay it all over again, he simply took a large mallet and banged the lump flat.

Just then in came the warty witch customer, carrying a tray. 'I've brought you a cup of tea,' she said. 'And you must have left these cigarettes in the other room. Oh, by the way, you haven't seen my little pet toad anywhere, have you?'

A warty wizard went into the police station one day and said that he wanted to make a complaint.

'I've got three brothers,' he explained, 'and we all live in one room. But one of my brothers has six goats. Another has six black cats. And the other

has a hundred rats. The smell in there is terrible. You must do something.'

'Hasn't your room got any windows?' asked the sergeant.

'Of course it has,' said the wizard.

'So why don't you open them?' said the policeman.

'What?' said the wizard, 'and lose all my bats?'

The Warty Witches' Fiendish Friends

Various Vampires

What do you get if you cross Dracula with a snail?
The world's slowest vampire.

What's a vampire's favourite animal?
A giraffe.

What do you get if you cross Dracula with Sir Lancelot?
A bite in shining armour.

What's Dracula's favourite coffee?
De-coffin-ated.

What's Dracula's car called?
A mobile blood unit.

Why do vampires do well at school?
Because every time they're asked a question, they come up with a biting reply.

POLICEMAN: What are you doing on this road, Dracula?
DRACULA: *Looking for the main artery, officer.*

What does a vampire bath in?
A bat tub.

What is pink, has a curly tail and drinks blood?
A hampire.

What do you get if you cross a Rolls Royce with a vampire?
A monster that attacks expensive cars and sucks out their petrol tanks.

How do you join the Dracula Fan Club?
Send your name, address, and blood group.

What is a vampire's favourite breakfast cereal?
Ready Neck.

Terrible Toads

Deep in the jungle there lived a very talkative,
wide-mouthed warty toad. He was always going
up to the other animals, asking them who they
were and what they did, then telling them, very
loudly and at great length, who *he* was.

One day the wide-mouthed warty toad went up
to a giant pink cat. 'Who are you and what do you
do?' asked the warty toad in his usual manner.

'I'm a giant pink cat and I miaow all day.'

'Oh, well I'm a wide-mouthed warty toad and I
talk loudly all day,' said the warty toad.

Further along the jungle track he came across
a python with two heads. 'Who are you and what
do you do?' asked the wide-mouthed warty toad.

'I'm a two-headed python and I hiss and slither all day.'

'Oh, well I'm a wide-mouthed warty toad and I talk loudly all day,' said the warty toad.

Then, right in the middle of the dark jungle, the warty toad met an enormous purple gorilla.

'Who are you and what do you do?' asked the wide-mouthed warty toad.

'I'm an enormous purple gorilla and I eat loud, wide-mouthed warty toads,' said the gorilla.

'Oh!' said the warty toad in a whisper, pursing his lips slightly. 'You don't see many of those about, do you?'

What ballet is most popular with warty toads?
Swamp Lake.

What is green and spins around at 100mph?
A toad in a liquidizer.

What do you get if you cross a galaxy with a toad?
Star Warts.

'Doctor, doctor, I feel like a toad!'
'Can't you see I'm busy — hop it.'

What do you get if you cross a muppet with a thick mist?
Kermit the Fog.

A warty toad walks into a café and orders a cup of tea.

'That'll be £1,' said the waitress when she brought it to him. 'You know I was just thinking, we don't get many warty toads in here.'

'I'm not surprised,' said the warty toad, 'with tea at £1 a cup!'

What do warty toads drink?
Croaka Cola.

Why did the warty toad eat candles?
For light refreshment.

What do you call a girl with a warty toad on her head?
Lily.

What is a warty toad's favourite sweet?
A lollihop.

What happened to the warty toad when it died?
The poor thing simply croaked.

What goes dot-dot-croak, croak-dot-dot, croak-croak-dot?
Morse toad.

What is a cloak?
The mating call of a Chinese warty toad.

What do you call a warty toad spy?
A croak and dagger agent.

What's the weakest animal in the world?
A warty toad. He will croak if you touch him.

Where do warty toads leave their hats and coats?
In the croakroom.

What is green and hard?
A warty toad with a machine gun.

What's green inside and white outside, and squelchy to eat?
A warty toad sandwich.

What happens to warty toads when they park on double yellow lines?
They get toad away.

'Orrible Owls

WARTY OWL: Us owls are a lot wiser than you chickens.
CHICKEN: *Oh yeah? What makes you so sure?*
WARTY OWL: Did you ever hear of Kentucky Fried Owl?

Knock, knock.
Who's there?
Owl.
Owl who?
Owl be sad if you don't let me in.

Knock, knock.
Who's there?
Owl.
Owl who?
Owl aboard the Skylark!

What do two lovesick warty owls say when it's raining?
Too-wet-to-woo.

Knock, knock.
Who's there?
Owl.
Owl who?
Owl I can say is 'Knock, knock'.

What sits in a tree and says, 'Hoots mon, hoots mon?'
A warty Scottish owl.

Slithery Snakes

What is a warty snake's favourite food?
Hiss fingers!

What's long and green and goes 'hith'?
A warty snake with a lisp.

Which hand would you use to grab a poisonous warty snake?
Your enemy's.

What is a warty snake's favourite opera?
Wriggletto.

Why did the two boa constrictors get married?
Because they had a crush on each other.

What do you get if you cross a warty snake with a Lego set?
A boa constructor.

What do you get if you cross a wild pig with a warty snake?
A boar constrictor.

What do you get if you cross a warty snake with a government employee?
A civil serpent.

What do you get if you cross an adder with a trumpet?
A warty snake in the brass.

What happened to the warty snake with a cold?
She adder viper nose.

What do you get if you cross a warty snake with a magic spell?
Addercadabra — or Abradacobra.

What happened when a deadly rattlesnake bit the warty witch?
It died in agony.

Beastly Bats

1ST WARTY WITCH (*just before a cricket match*):
How do you hold a bat?
2ND WARTY WITCH: *By the wings, of course!*

What do warty witches' children like to play?
Bat's cradle!

What happened to the two vampires who were insane?
They went bats.

What animal is the best cricket player?
The bat.

What does a warty bat sing in the rain?
'Raindrops Keep Falling On My Feet.'

VICTIM: A warty witch's bat bit me on the neck
last night.
FRIEND: *Did you put anything on it?*
VICTIM: No, it seemed to like it as it was.

Scuttling Spiders

Knock, knock.
Who's there?
Webster.
Webster who?
Webster Spin, the warty spider.

What do you call an Irish warty spider?
Paddy Longlegs.

What's a warty spider's favourite television programme?
The Newly-Web Game.

CUSTOMER: Waiter, there's a warty spider in my soup. Send me the manager.
WAITER: *That's no good, sir, he's frightened of them too.*

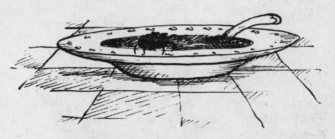

TEACHER: What did Robert the Bruce do after watching the warty spider climbing up and down?
PUPIL: *He went and invented the yo-yo.*

What did Mrs Warty-Spider say when Mr Warty-Spider broke her new web?
'Darn it!'

What did the warty spider say to the beetle?
'Stop bugging me.'

What are warty spiders' webs good for?
Warty spiders.

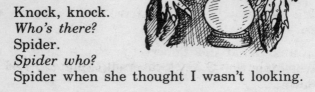

Knock, knock.
Who's there?
Spider.
Spider who?
Spider when she thought I wasn't looking.

Where do warty spiders live?
Crawley.

Creepy Cats

What is a warty black cat's favourite TV programme?
Miami Mice.

What's furry, has whiskers, and chases outlaws?
A posse cat.

Ding dong bell,
Pussy's in the well.
But we've put some disinfectant down,
And don't care about the smell!

What do warty black cats strive for?
Purr-fection.

Why did the warty black cat want to join the Red Cross?
It wanted to be a first aid kit.

Why was the warty black cat so small?
The warty witch fed her condensed milk.

When is it bad luck to be followed by a warty black cat?
When you're a mouse.

What is an octopus?
An eight-sided cat.

What noise does a warty black cat make going down the M1?
Miaoooooooooooooooooooooooooooooooooooooow!

Why do warty black cats never shave?
Because eight out of ten cats prefer Whiskas.

What did the warty black cat say to the fish-head?
I've got a bone to pick with you.

A woman was walking behind a hearse with a big
warty witch's cat on a lead. Behind them stretched
a long line of mourners.
'What happened?' asked a passer-by.
'The warty witch's cat bit my husband, and he
died of fright.'
'Can I borrow it?' the passer-by asked.
The woman pointed behind her. 'Get in the
queue,' she said.

What do you call a warty black cat that sucks acid
drops?
A sour puss.

Now you see it, now you don't — what is it?
A warty black cat walking over a zebra crossing.

What has four legs, a tail, whiskers and flies?
A dead warty black cat.

What has four legs, a tail, whiskers and can't stand still?
A warty black cat in a tumble-drier.

What has four legs, a tail, whiskers and cuts grass?
A lawn-miaower.

What do you get if you cross a warty black cat and a canary?
A satisfied warty black cat and a dead canary.

What do you call a warty cat with no legs?
It doesn't matter what you call him, he still won't come.

The Warty Witches' Fearsome Finale

What's evil and ugly and goes up and down?
A warty witch in a lift.

Two warty witches lost their brooms and crashlanded on an iceberg. 'Do you think we'll be here long?' asked the first.
  'No,' said the second, 'here comes the Titanic.'

What is evil and ugly and noisy?
A warty witch with a set of drums.

What is evil and ugly with red spots?
A warty witch with measles.

When a warty witch falls into a lake, what is the first thing she does?
Gets wet.

What is evil and ugly and goes round and round?
A warty witch in a revolving door.

What is evil and ugly on the inside, and green on the outside?
A warty witch disguised as a cucumber.

What is evil and ugly and bounces?
A warty witch on a pogo-stick.

What is evil and ugly and goes at 125mph?
A warty witch on an Inter-City train.

What happened to West Brom-witch Albion?
They had a spell in the First Division.

Have you heard about the weather witch?
She's forecasting sunny spells.

Two witches came out of the theatre one night.
One said to the other, 'Shall we walk home, or
shall we take a broom?'

Why did the warty witch put her broom in the
washing machine?
She wanted a clean sweep.

What's a warty witch's favourite book?
Broom at the Top.

What's the warty witches' favourite pop group?
Broomski Beat.

Why did the warty witch join Tottenham Hotspur?
She heard they needed a new sweeper.

How do we know Bob Geldof is a warty witch?
Because he started the Broomtown Rats.

Why were the warty witches on strike?
They wanted sweeping reforms.

WARTY WITCH: I'd like a new frog, please.
PET SHOP ASSISTANT: *But you only bought one yesterday. What happened?*
WARTY WITCH: It Kermit-ted suicide.

Why do warty witches ride broomsticks?
Because their vacuum cleaner leads are too short.

What do you call a warty witch who goes to the beach but is too scared to go for a swim in the sea?
A chicken sand-witch.

Who went into the warty witch's den and came out alive?
The warty witch.

What do you call two warty witches who share a broom?
Broom-mates.

What do warty witches use pencil sharpeners for?
To keep their hats pointed.

Knock, knock.
Who's there?
Ivy.
Ivy who?
Ivy cast a spell on you!

If a flying saucer is an aircraft, does that make a broomstick a witchcraft?

How do warty witches tell the time?
They use their witch watches.

What's the best way of talking to a warty witch?
By telephone.

What do warty witches like to read in the newspaper?
Their horror-scopes.

WARTY WITCH IN SHOE SHOP: I'd like a pair of sandals, please.
SHOP ASSISTANT: *Certainly, madam, what kind?*
WARTY WITCH: Open-toad, of course!

How can you tell an Italian warty witch from a Scottish one?
By her suntan.

Why did the warty witch climb Nelson's Column?
To get her kite.

Why did the warty witch go over the mountain?
She couldn't go under it.

Why did the warty witch dye her hair yellow?
To see if it's true that blondes have more fun.

'The police are looking for a warty witch with one eye.'
'*Why don't they use two?*'

Why did the warty witch wear a green felt pointed hat?
So she could walk across snooker tables without being seen.

Why do warty witches scratch themselves?
They're the only ones that know where they itch.

What do you get if you cross a warty witch with peanut butter?
A warty witch that sticks to the roof of your mouth.

What is evil and ugly and lives under the sea?
A warty witch with an aqualung.

What do you get if you cross a river with an inflatable warty witch?
To the other side.

What is the first thing a warty witch does in the morning?
She wakes up.

1ST WARTY WITCH: I'm so unlucky.
2ND WARTY WITCH: *Why's that?*
1ST WARTY WITCH: I met a handsome prince at a party but when I kissed him he turned into a frog.

Why do warty witches get stiff joints?
They catch broomatism.

What would happen to a warty witch if she swallowed a frog?
She might croak.

What do racing witches ride on?
Vroomsticks.

What name did the warty witch give to her cooking pot?
It was called-Ron.

What would a warty witch do if she wanted to diet?
She'd go to Weight Witches.

Terror in Transylvania

A man was stranded miles from anywhere in Transylvania, on a cold and stormy night. He could just make out a light in the distance, and he followed it until he came to a weird and creepy old castle.

The owner offered him a bed for the night, but warned him that there was a trapdoor in the middle of his bedroom floor which he must not open *under any circumstances*.

In the middle of the night, however, the man's curiosity got the better of him. Grasping the handle of the trapdoor, he slowly pulled it open. A terrible smell attacked the man's nostrils as he peered into the inky blackness of the pit below, but he could see nothing.

Very gingerly, he lowered his arm into hole, feeling around in the clammy darkness. It was then that he touched it . . . a horrible, cold, slimy lump

of matter . . . that suddenly came to life and groaned.

Screaming with terror, the man jumped up and ran out into the storm-lashed night. But as fast as he moved, the evil, ugly, slimy, warty witch kept pace, and, if anything, was gaining slowly.

To his relief, the man found a rowing boat by the side of a lake, and he pushed it away from the bank and jumped in. He rowed furiously, peering frantically behind him into the darkness of the alien night for a glimpse of the hideous creature that was pursuing him.

At first, he thought he had escaped, but then he heard the splashes, and knew, with a heavy heart, that the game was up. But driven by an incredibly powerful instinct for preservation, the man rowed and rowed until his hands were raw and his very last ounce of strength had been exhausted. Near collapse, he steered the boat on to the far bank and fell on to the cold, dank earth to await his fate.

He could only watch in horror as the horrible, evil, ugly, slimy, warty witch reared out of the water and bore down on him. The stench as she approached was beyond words. Then, just inches from where the terror-stricken man lay, the evil, ugly, slimy, warty witch stopped . . . stretched out a fearsome six-inch-long finger-nail, and cackled: 'Caught you! You're *it*! Na, na, na-na, na!'

What lies at the bottom of the sea and shakes?

A NURVOUS warty witch.